THE DAPPY A_ _
OF DIPPY DAN

DIPPY AND THE WHALE

Bible stories told rather differently

By Dan Carlton

Preface.

Children in this modern age have been deprived of many things but especially the ability to make good, informed decisions in later life with regard to their spiritual well-being. This series of Dippy Dan Bible stories attempts in part to address this deficiency in the lives of so many children who may for whatever reason, be deprived of the great stories of the Bible. By introducing them via our own wonderful Dippy Dan Character who although amazingly intelligent, has the capacity to do the Dippiest things imaginable that get him into all kinds of trouble. We hope and pray that by God's Grace they may grow up to remember these timeless stories and in doing so come to understand something of the loving heart of God for all who will take the time to seek Him.

Mission Statement.

The Author is a retired Christian Missionary who has spent more than forty years ministering to children at home and abroad.

For centuries, the great truths of the Bible have been portrayed via art, music, drama and in modern times through movies and internet games etc. So, using a cartoon character like Dippy Dan has given us an opportunity to enable children everywhere to identify with Dippy's antics and behaviour but whilst the adventures of Dippy Dan are naturally fiction and fun, our sincere intention is not to trivialise the main reason for using this cartoon media but to teach children something about the Holy Bible from the wonderful stories therein and in turn let them enjoy Dippy's exciting adventures.

We wish all who come into contact with the adventures of Dippy Dan to be made aware that we believe the stories of the Bible to be true and we desire that children would somehow find out for themselves what these truths mean in this Godless generation.

Were it possible to reach children some other way, solely via Church activities then this great work would not be necessary and so we endeavour to provide an additional alternative that is both fun and informative for children and of course for the Glory of God.

The Dappy Adventures of Dippy Dan
First published in Great Britain in 2018 by:

Dippy Dan Books
Faversham
Kent

Credits:
Special thanks are given to my wife Anita who has endured hundreds of hours of my absence, her patience and loving support has made this work possible.

Thanks also to my Daughter Maria Carlton (See Photo of us both on back of book) who is an awesome, talented communicator and marketing professional. She has faithfully and diligently edited and proofread this work, tirelessly working with me to get Dippy Dan Books into the hearts of children around the world.

Acknowledgements:
We are proud to promote the beautiful, inspirational children's Bible resources that Friends and Heroes produce to all our Dippy Dan readers worldwide.

Find Friends and Heroes on these two websites below:
www.friendsandheroes.com
www.friendsandheroes.tv

Contents

Chapter   Page

1. School's out but there's trouble ahead..............6

2. Dippy needs his Mum's cooperation..................12

3. Plans are meant to be changed, right?.............17

4. Fixing stone dogs is hard, can you do it?...........22

5. The story of Jonah get's Dippy excited...............28

6. Dippy gone to sea and guess who he sees?.......33

7. Who ever thought Whales are smelly? 39

8. Free! But Can Dippy find his BTTM remote?.......43

9. Time travel can solve many problems!................49

10. Is Dippy falling in love with Oggia?.....................55

INTRODUCTION:

In Dippy Dan's first adventure we read that Dippy had discovered a secret cave on a small deserted island while on holiday and when he went deep inside the cave he found a big green time machine. Dippy entered the time machine and found to his amazement that he was able to travel back in time to some amazing places, to meet some very interesting people!
Things just get a whole lot better in Dippy's second adventure when his Uncle Sid finds a very special remote controller that can give Dippy total control of his BGTM, to make it appear and disappear back to his Dippy cave whenever he wants it to!

Join Dippy Dan again on this, his third adventure.

Chapter One

Dippy Dan's alarm clock suddenly went off and before he could slam his hand down to stop it ringing his Mum shouted up the stairs.

"Get up Dippy it's time for school." Dippy looked at his clock, it was time to get up all right!

"Oh Muuum," he moaned loudly under his breath. The bedroom door opened and in came Dippy's Mummy. "Heard that," she said with a smile.

"I was dreaming about time travel Mum," said Dippy rubbing his eyes and yawning.

"Never mind time travel, you need to travel downstairs for your breakfast before you run out of time." Dippy grumbled and said, "Going to school isn't as much fun as time travel though Mum."

Every morning was the same in Dippy Dan's house with his Mum rushing around the kitchen table, making sure Dippy's Dad, his two sisters Poppy and Sue and of course Dylan his brother had their breakfast and her three children had their lunch boxes in their school bag and that their faces were clean.

"Everyone ready then?" she would ask.

"Yes Mum!" would come the answer from Dippy, his two sisters and brother. "Off you go then," said Mum, while Dippy hung back in the kitchen with his fingers in the syrup.

"Hurry Dippy you'll miss the bus if you don't get a move on." And off they went to catch their bus.

"Bye Mum," they would all shout together as they rushed out of the front door like a whirlwind leaving their Mummy exhausted but happy that they had just one last day before the summer holiday and she could put her feet up for a while with a nice cup of tea but it would soon be time to clear up the mess the kids had made.

When Dippy got to school he drew his Teacher on the blackboard and sat down at his desk then he made a paper airplane and threw it over everyone's head but then suddenly the door opened and the airplane flew straight into his Teacher's nose, "gotcha!" whispered Dippy.

"Right, who threw that?" cried Dippy's teacher and of course no one owned up but then the teacher's pet shouted out, "It was Dippy Sir, I saw him throw it and I saw him draw that silly picture of you on the blackboard."

Dippy looked across and poked his tongue out. Mr Brown's face went bright red with rage and he bellowed, "Now Dippy Dan my lad, you will be punished by writing a five page story and you will stay here until it is finished."

Dippy couldn't help smiling to himself and guess what he was going to write about? Yep you got it, time travel of course, what else!

Dippy began his story by choosing Jonah and the Whale, a Bible story that he loved his Mummy to read to him and he wrote and wrote and wrote until he had finished all five pages, which was his punishment for throwing a paper airplane at his Teacher.

All the children in the class were still busy doing their work but Dippy had finished and just sat there grinning From ear to ear?

"What are you smiling about young man?" boomed Mr. Brown, Dippy Dan answered,

"I've finished my story Sir, can I come show you?"

Everyone looked at Dippy with shock because no one could believe that he would get so much hard work done in such a short time but then Dippy Dan was writing about his favorite subject.... time travel obviously!

"Bring the work here boy," said Dippy's Teacher and Mr. Brown read Dippy's story with interest.

"Whale ay?" he said and handed it back to Dippy and mumbled, "I guess it will do." so Dippy Dan went back to his seat grinning at everyone.

"At last," whispered Dippy as Mr. Brown opened the door to let all the children go home.

As they went through the door his Teacher looked down at Dippy, gave him a warm smile and said,

"Well done my boy" and without looking up at Mr. Brown, Dippy said, "Thank you Sir," and off Dippy skipped all the way home but he wasn't going to tell his Mummy what had happened in school that day... would you?

School's out and Dippy has decided where he wants to go in his BGTM but first he needs to get his Mum and Dad to agree to help him do something… but what is his plan?

Chapter Two

Dippy Dan got home and after his tea he said to his Mum, "Can I go and play please Mum?"

She answered, "As long as you remember where you live," then shook her head and added,

"Just be a good boy, you know what I mean Dippy, get back before your Daddy comes home from work, ok?"

Dippy waved his hand as he ran out into the garden and climbed on his bike pretending to go for a ride, so that his Mum wouldn't become suspicious!

"Ok Mummy," he said, "See you later then," and disappeared into his Dippy cave where he had hidden something very special… Only we know what that is!

Checking that no one was coming, Dippy lifted the brown tarpaulin off his BGTM which brought a rush of excitement to his heart because he knew that there wasn't any place or time he couldn't go to, he could even go to other planets and stars if he wanted to.

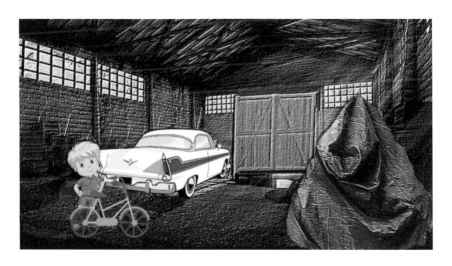

But Dippy had set his heart on visiting all the amazing people in the Bible that he had heard about. Great people like Noah and even Adam and Eve!

Now where shall I go next? Ah I know, thought Dippy, remembering the story of Jonah and the Whale he wrote about at school.

Right, he decided, I'll go and visit Jonah and then imagined all the fun he would have inside a big smelly Whale. But first I need to see if Mummy will let me camp out in the old garage tomorrow night, otherwise she will wonder where I have disappeared to and get worried about me, just like Mum's do.

That evening after Dippy's Dad got home and was sitting by the fire reading his paper, Dippy asked,

"Daddy can I ask you something important?" his Dad looked up from his paper and frowning said,

"Hmm, that sounds like you want me to do something for you." Dippy shrugged his shoulders and screwed up his nose and said,

"You know you don't use the old garage any more since the new one was built?"

"Yes," answered his Dad. "Well," said Dippy,

"Could I have the old garage as my Dippy cave?"

Dippy Dan's Dad looked at him with a twinkle in his eye and said, "You mean like a man-cave?"

Dippy replied with one of his serious faces,

"Yeah, that's it Dad just like a man-cave but my own Dippy cave."

The silence that followed made Dippy think that his Dad would say no but then he put his paper down and said,

"Ok, I will let you use the old garage as a Dippy cave but it will be up to you to sort out all the rubbish and that old car will have to stay there, ok?" Dippy Dan was so happy that he hugged his Daddy.

"That's a deal Dad," said Dippy.

So, Dippy became the proud owner of his own Dippy cave and Time Machine hanger and straight away put a notice on the big double doors saying,

'No trespassing and no uninvited guests!' That was so that his sisters and brother wouldn't discover his secret.

The next day Dippy came up with a plan and his Mummy knew that meant trouble but she sat and listened to his great plan, which was to take his big green tent and camp out overnight inside his new Dippy cave, his Mum said,

"Ok Dippy you can camp out tonight in your Dippy cave but if you get scared you must come back indoors." Dippy smiles and replied, "Ok Mummy I promise."

But Dippy knew that he was going to be far too busy to get scared and besides he was looking forward to going back in time to see Jonah and his big Whale.

Time for a tidy up in here, better close the big double doors first, thought Dippy as he walked around his new Dippy cave.

"Right, I can put my tent up here and I can lean my bike on Dad's old car," he muttered.

The garage was big enough to do lots of things and was just right as a time machine hanger.

Dippy climbed inside his green tent.

"I'll get some rest before I start out," muttered Dippy, as though he was talking to someone.

He lay there in his tent with his eyes tightly shut and tried to get some sleep but it was hopeless, he was just too excited so he got back up again.

Dippy Dan stood looking all thoughtful and said,

I think I will try and go somewhere different before teatime and then I will be ready for my big adventure to see Jonah, he thought. So, he opened the door of his BGTM went in and sat down and got himself comfortable.

Right then, where shall I go? he wondered.

Dippy Dan always has a plan but it never always goes quite right and his sudden good idea to change his plan lands him in a strange place where he meets Oggia. But who is she...

Chapter Three

Oh, I know, I'll go back to the Stone Age where Fred Flintstone and Barney Rubble came from and see if I can find some new friends.

So, Dippy closed the door, set the controls and off he went whirling through space and time, all the way back to the Stone Age. The time machine landed with a bump and Dippy carefully opened the door to have a look around.

"What's this?" he muttered under his breath,
"A Caveman's cave and it looks like there's no one home, I'll go and have a look around."

Dippy thought maybe he should send his BGTM back to his Dippy cave before anyone sees it and quickly took out his BGTM remote controller and in a flash his time machine was gone way off into the future and back to his Dippy cave in Carltonville.

"It's time to go and see what's out there. Perhaps Fred Flintstone lives here," he giggled to himself.

There on the floor were bones, lots of fluffy looking animal skin clothes and a small fire burning brightly near the opening with a pot of boiling food on top.

The Cavemen must be out hunting, thought Dippy and so he popped his head out of the cave to check that it was all clear for him to go exploring.

I'de better be careful cos I know that cavemen are savages and would be very angry if they found me here, he thought so carefully and slowly he wandered out from the mouth of the cave and there in front of him was a little cave girl sitting on a rock crying. Dippy tiptoed up to her and saw that she was trying to fix her broken stone toy which looked like a Doggy and was all in pieces on the floor.

When Dippy got to the little girl she suddenly turned and screamed but Dippy held out his hands and smiled at her and at first she was very scared to see such a strange looking boy.

Gradually Dippy was able to make her understand that he wasn't going to hurt her and pointed to himself and said,

"Me Dippy Dan."

The little cave girl looked puzzled but bit by bit she realised that Dippy Dan was telling her his name and she stopped crying, pointed to herself and uttered what sounded like "Oggia," so Dippy took her hand and said,

"Hello Oggia, my name is Dippy Dan." The little cave girl mimicked Dippy and grunted,

"Ippy Yan." Dippy wasn't going to be able to actually speak to her in his own language but with his language gizmo, his hands waving and by pulling funny faces they were soon able to at least make each other understood.

"What's up," he said, wiping a tear from her face.

The little girl pointed to her stone toy and she began to cry again, she didn't seem to be scared of Dippy Dan at all now and soon both of them were working out how to fix the stone doggy.

Dippy would put one bit there and the little girl would shake her head so he would try putting a piece somewhere else, then she would smile as if to show Dippy that it was in the right place but then when the doggy was all back together, it would just fall apart again and the little girl would start crying again.

So Dippy had an idea and he took the little girl by the hand and led her into her cave, took out his BGTM remote and in a flash his time machine appeared and Dippy opened the big green door.

The little Cave girl's eyes were wide with wonder and as all little boys know that anything can happen at any time and so a bag of tools and bits and bobs, screws, string and glue are always important things to carry with you, even in a time machine!

Look carefully at the pictures below and see if you can find where all the mixed up broken bits fit onto the stone dog.

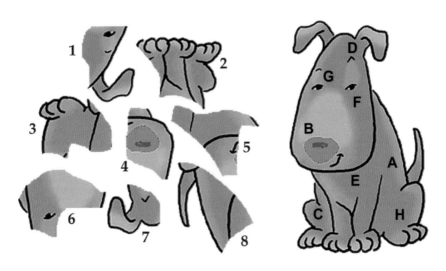

While Dippy was getting all that he needed to fix Oggia's stone dog, he couldn't help wondering how many other people he would be able to help by going back in time to places where simple things like glue hadn't yet been invented and decided there and then to try and help as many people as he could.

There were so many times back home in his own time when Dippy saw that someone needed help and even though he always hoped to get some sweets in return, he always stopped to help.

One time he saw an old lady fall off her bicycle and seeing that there wasn't anyone around, Dippy ran to the rescue and wrapped his wooly scarf around the old lady's knee because it was bleeding. She called at Dippy's house with a big bag of fruit much to Dippy's disappointment because he would have like sweets instead but he was glad he helped her.

Find out next time if Dippy can fix Oggia's stone Doggy and why he plans to come back.

Chapter Four

So Dippy took the tube of glue and his big white work sheet out from his BGTM tool bag and went back outside the cave with Oggia.

Dippy laid out his work sheet on the floor and put all the broken Doggy pieces on top and carefully glued them into place until the doggy was mended and the little girl smiled and giggled.

She was so happy to have her toy back again and Dippy Dan was happy too because he knew that the little cave girl would never have been able to fix her stone doggy by herself.

In the distance, Dippy Dan could see someone was coming and turning to get a better look, he noticed it was a Cave lady dragging an animal skin full of water from the river below and Dippy guessed it must be Oggia's Mummy but he knew he couldn't do anything right there and then to help her get the water any easier, besides she may be angry with him if she saw him there. "If only I had more time, there must be a better way of carrying the water up from the river to the cave.

Then Dippy thought, Maybe when I get home I can think of a better way to help Oggia's Mummy to get the water from the river without all that hard work and then I can come back and help them.

Dippy really loved Oggia and couldn't wait to get back home to think up a plan to help her Mummy.

"I had better get going or I'll be late for tea. I'm really going to miss Oggia thought Dippy to himself."

Dippy took the little girl's hands in his and they both smiled at each other.

"Goodbye," he said happily and even though the little girl couldn't understand what Dippy was saying or what a time machine was, she knew that Dippy liked her and was going to have to leave her before her Mummy came home.

They both stood smiling at each other then Dippy went in and closed the door to his BGTM and shouted,

"See you again I hope Oggia" and they waved frantically to each other. Then off went Dippy back to his Dippy cave thousands of years into the future, hopefully just in time for tea!

Landing in his Dippy cave was a bit bumpy but Dippy had arrived back home safely and went into the house where his Mummy stood waiting for him.

"Wash your hands before you have your tea Dippy," ordered his Mum and so Dippy Dan sat down to eat with his family.

"Have you had a nice afternoon?" enquired his Mummy.

"Oh yes Mum, I went to visit a little girl from the Stone Age and I fixed her stone doggy with some glue."

Dippy looked into his Mum's face, she was smiling but with her mouth open and her eyes wide with wonder because she just didn't believe him.

Dippy's Mummy turned and looked at Dippy's Dad, smiled again and said,

"That's nice Dippy, eat your food then." Dippy could see that no one believed him but it didn't matter because he knew it was true and that was all that mattered.

Dippy finished his tea and got all the things together that he needed to stay overnight in his Dippy cave. His Mum told him to take his Teddy and a bottle of water with him, like Mum's do and not to forget to brush his teeth.

"I will bring you some hot chocolate later and read you a story before you settle down."

"Ok Mum, see you later and don't worry I'll be fine," said Dippy pulling a funny face.

He hugged his Mummy and Daddy and waved goodnight to his two sisters and his brother and went excitedly out to his Dippy cave knowing that it was going to be a long night full of adventure, danger and fun.

When Dippy got back to his Dippy cave he wondered what he was going to do with his time machine because his Mummy was soon going to arrive and he couldn't risk her asking too many questions even though it was covered with the brown tarpaulin.

So, Dippy took out his BGTM remote and sent his time machine behind the trees at the end of the garden just in case and at the very moment his time machine vanished, his Mummy came in through the double doors. Then, Dippy quickly ran over to his bike and fiddled with the wheels, spinning them and checking the tyres.

"Are you alright Dippy," she said and gave Dippy his cup of hot chocolate.

"Er, yeah Mum I'm cool, just checking my bike tyres are up ready for tomorrow." Naughty ol Dippy telling porky pies to his mum!

"Now you get inside your sleeping bag," she said,

"And I will tell you a story. Which story would you like me to read to you tonight?"

Dippy pretended to think for a minute and then said with a long, loud yawn,

"Can you read me the story of Jonah and the Whale please Mum?"

"Yes of course I can Dippy, I just hope you won't ever be as naughty as Jonah was."

"Who me?" answered Dippy, with a sly grin on his face. If only his Mummy knew!

"No not me Mum, I'm always a good boy you know that and besides, there are no Whales around here."

They both laughed but Dippy's Mummy didn't know that her little boy would soon be far away in another time... being swallowed by a Whale!

"Settle down then and I will tell you the story of Jonah and the Whale from your little blue bible.

Dippy looked into his Mummy's face and felt such love for her. She was always there to look after him and to make sure that he was safe and happy and Dippy thought of all the children out there who had no one to love them and no one to tell them such wonderful Bible stories!

Dippy's Mummy knew that it was very important that Dippy grew up to know that God loved him and that no matter what happened to him in his life, God would always be there to look after him.

Dippy's Mummy opened the Bible and began to read from the book of Jonah and she kept looking at Dippy with her big blue loving eyes, glad that her little Dippy was such a good boy... but we know different!

Chapter Five

One day God asked a man named Jonah to go to a place called Nineveh and tell the people living there to stop being bad. The only problem was that Jonah didn't want to help the people there.

He knew they were bad and he wanted them to be punished for their mistakes.

So instead of listening to God, Jonah thought he would run away from Nineveh and not do what God asked him. He ran to the sea where he found a ship that was going to another city. He paid the captain, went in the lower part of the boat and went to sleep.

Shortly after the boat left the shore, a very bad storm came up and started tossing the boat around. All the men were very afraid so they started to throw all their packages and bags overboard in hopes that they wouldn't drown.

The captain soon went to find Jonah who was still sound asleep in the boat. He said to Jonah,

"How can you sleep? Get up and pray to your god, maybe he can help us!" The captain didn't realise that Jonah didn't just believe in any God but the one true God, as only He could help them.

Meanwhile, the other sailors decided that the storm was Jonah's fault. He must have done something wrong to make his god so angry. So they asked Jonah.

"What have you done? What god do you believe in? What can we do to make this storm stop?"

Jonah told them, "I believe in the Lord, the God of heaven, who made the sea and the land and I am running away from something God asked me to do. It is my fault this is happening. If you throw me into the sea the storm will stop."

The men didn't want to hurt Jonah by throwing him off the boat so they tried to row the best they could, but the storm just got worse. So eventually they picked up Jonah and threw him into the sea. The storm immediately calmed and the sea became still. The men on the boat realised that Jonah believed in the one true God and prayed to Him.

Then the captain and the crew looked out to sea as a huge Whale (The Bible says it was a fish) came and swallowed up Jonah. God actually sent the Whale to keep Jonah from drowning. Jonah stayed in the Whale's belly for three days and three nights.

Just think for a second what it would be like to be inside a Whale. There are no windows and lots of strange things floating around that you can't see because it's so dark.

Other than that, I'm not sure what it would be like, but Jonah probably didn't know if he would ever see daylight again.

While Jonah was trapped inside the Whale he did a lot of praying to God. He asked God to forgive him for running away. He also thanked God for not allowing him to drown.

After the third day God told the Whale to spit Jonah out onto dry land. And the Whale did just that. Jonah was happy to be out of the dark belly of the Whale, but boy, did he need a shower. He was all slimy and smelly. Yuck!

Then the Lord told Jonah a second time to go to Nineveh and tell the people there to stop being bad. This time Jonah obeyed God and left for Nineveh right away.

When Jonah got there he told the people what had happened to him. He warned them that God said they should stop doing bad things or in forty days the city and everything in it would be destroyed. To Jonah's surprise the people listened to him and they prayed to God and said sorry for all the bad things they had done.

Soon the king of Nineveh heard what was going on and he ordered that everyone was to listen to God and to stop doing bad things. When God saw that they were trying to do good instead of bad He felt love for them and did not destroy their city.

That could be the end of the story except Jonah left the city very angry. He was mad that God didn't punish the people but he also knew that God was a loving God and didn't want to destroy anything if He doesn't have to.

So, Jonah went up on a hill and sulked. God saw Jonah and knew how he was feeling so he explained to Jonah that He loves everyone (after all he made us). He told him that He doesn't like to punish people who are doing bad things, God would rather see us make the choice to turn from our bad ways and do good again.

End of Bible story.

———————————

Dippy's Mum finished reading the story, closed the Bible and whispered,

"Good night Dippy, now you get some sleep and remember if you get scared you can come straight back indoors."

"Sure Mum but don't worry I'll be alright, good night." After his Mummy had gone Dippy opened the door of his BGTM and closed the door behind him.

"Time to go and find Jonah then," he muttered, knowing no one was there to hear him!

Dippy made the necessary adjustments, set the time and slide his key-card into the slot and off he went!

Dippy finds himself on a ship being blown by a terrible storm across the sea and guess what he thinks of first? Yep, you got it, his belly. Dippy is hungry, but can he find anything to eat?

Chapter Six

The next moment Dippy crash-landed his BGTM somewhere and was being tossed back and forth inside his time machine and couldn't understand what was happening.

When Dippy slowly opened the door he saw that he was inside a big wooden ship being thrown about by a big storm and when Dippy looked out of the ship's porthole, he saw there were great big waves crashing over the ship. Oh dear, I hope that this is the right place, wondered Dippy.

Luckily for Dippy his time machine had stopped behind a stack of boxes so no one could see it there. And after he made a few adjustments on his BGTM remote it disappeared back to his Dippy cave.

Now it was time to go exploring. First Dippy needed to find some food and so he followed his nose and sure enough his nose led him straight to the ship's kitchen. Thankfully because the storm was so strong there weren't any cooks working.

So Dippy sneaked in and found a big bunch of grapes and walked around munching them.

He opened all the cupboards to see if he could find anything else worth eating and found bowls of Monkey nuts and began stuffing them carefully into his pockets.   After a while Dippy decided to abandon his search for nice food like biscuits and cakes and went exploring instead.

This ship must be where Jonah is, thought Dippy, I'll go and look for him, better be careful though.

Dippy Dan knew from the Bible stories his Mum had told him that Jonah had run away from God and got onto a ship to escape from doing what God asked him to do but everything went wrong for him after that.

The ship was being thrown around in the storm and because it was night-time Dippy couldn't see much except for the little oil lamps in the long corridors that shone to show him where he was going.

Of course it was very hard for Dippy Dan to walk around without being pushed one way and then the other as the waves crashed against the side of the Ship making it very hard to walk in a straight line.

All of a sudden Dippy saw a man coming along the narrow corridor towards him so he hid inside a little room where there were some funny hanging beds.

Dippy climbed into one of them and covered himself up with an old sheet. Luckily the Sailor passed by without seeing Dippy hiding.

"Phew that was close, better go and look for Jonah again," muttered Dippy and there laying fast asleep down on the storeroom floor behind some old sacks was Jonah, right there where his BGTM had landed.

Dippy sat on an old sack remembering the story of Jonah and the Whale that his Mum had read to him and knew that Jonah had fallen asleep in the cargo Storeroom of the ship, suddenly Jonah started to wake up and opened his eyes. Dippy said,

"Hi, my name is Dippy Dan," Jonah answered,

"Well you are just a small boy, how did you get in here?" Dippy told him that he got there in his big green time machine which can travel through space and time. Jonah gave a great big yawn and said,

"Now tell me the truth, how did you get down here?" So Dippy fibbed and said, "I wanted to learn to be a Fisherman and I sneaked on board the ship when no one was looking," Jonah shook his head and yawned again and said,

"Ok, it doesn't matter, we need to make sure you don't get caught or the Captain will throw you over the side which is what they do to all Stowaways!"

So Dippy and Jonah spoke for a while and Dippy checked in his pocket that his BGTM remote was still there because the ship was being thrown all over the place. Thankfully his amazing tiny remote was safe.

He couldn't even imagine what would happen if he lost it somewhere because he would never be able to return to his own time.

Just as Dippy was clambering over the big sacks in the storeroom he fell and landed onto one of the soft sacks not realising that his BGTM remote had slipped out of his pocket and had fallen out. I can only imagine what will happen next, can you?

Dippy Dan is either very brave or very silly but I will leave that for you to decide, because what happens to him next will put Dippy in terrible danger....and very smelly too!

Chapter Seven

All of a sudden angry faces appeared at the top of the stairs and the Sailors shouted,

"Hey you two come up here!" And so Jonah and Dippy Dan climbed up the wooden steps trembling with fear and the Captain said to Dippy,

"You have stowed aboard and there is only one punishment for Stowaways." Dippy looked at Jonah, who had told him what they would do to him if they caught him. The Sailors surrounded him and looked so fierce and Dippy was very frightened of them!

"Throw him over the side," shouted one Sailor and another said,

"We'll have no Stowaways here." So they grabbed Dippy and... Sploosh, down he went into the wild stormy sea.

"Help!" cried Dippy, "Help me, please help me!" he shouted, but no one was coming to rescue him, not even Jonah.

Suddenly, over the top came Jonah too and down, down, down they both went into the depths of the sea. Dippy wanted his Mummy more than at any time in his life... wouldn't you?

Then, out of nowhere appeared a massive black Whale who opened its big great mouth to swallow Dippy Dan and Jonah.

The great big black Whale gave a big 'Gulp' and Dippy and Jonah went flying down his throat and into his belly. They landed upside down on top of each other somewhere deep inside the Whale. Then they stood there in utter shock as the Whale closed his mouth!

Thankfully, Jonah had some soggy rock cakes in his bag and Dippy had all those Monkey nuts he took from the ship's kitchen and so they shared what they had together, wondering how they were ever going to get out of their smelly prison.

Dippy said to Jonah, "Well I've told you how I got here but how did you get here?" And so Jonah began to tell Dippy Dan his own sad story, Dippy already knew of course but It was very special to hear it from the man himself!

Dippy decided that he wasn't going to stay for the three whole days that the Bible says Noah was there for, and so he told Noah about his time machine and that he could call it to take him out of there but Noah didn't believe him.

"Look, I'll prove it to you," said Dippy and reached into his pocket to get his BGTM remote and cried,

"Oh help! my BGTM remote has gone!"

"Don't worry Dippy, I'm sure it will turn up," answered Noah sarcastically. But Dippy wasn't listening because he knew that without it he would never be able to get back home.

"You don't understand Noah, I am stuck here and I can never go back to my family."

Dippy's head was bowed down with sadness and he began to cry and wanted his Mummy.

When Dippy looked up again, he saw that Noah was praying and even though Dippy believed in God, it was hard to believe that without his BGTM remote he could get back home again but hoped that somehow God would hear his new friend's prayers and answer him from deep down at the bottom of the ocean!

"Cheer up young Dippy," said Noah, "Well get out of here somehow and even though Dippy Knew they would, he couldn't make Noah understand that he was truly a prisoner, lost in the wrong time forever!

Dippy finally escapes from the smelly belly of the big Whale and has learned that sometimes what looks like a terrible mess, can turn out to be a lesson that you never forget!

Chapter Eight

Jonah loved Dippy and they talked and laughed and even cried together and after three days the big black Whale opened his mouth, gave a massive burp and spat Dippy and Jonah up onto the beach.

"Wow that was amazing," said Dippy.

"We are on dry land at last." So off they walked just like nothing had happened!

"Bye bye mister Whale," shouted Dippy as they walked off, thankful that they were safe and free at last, even though Dippy was still very upset!

Jonah and Dippy Dan had become great friends and Jonah told Dippy that no matter what happens he must trust that God will keep him safe and to always say sorry for the wrong things he had done.

"All this trouble has come to me," said Jonah,

"Because I wouldn't do what God told me to do but now I am going to Nineveh to do what God commanded me, it may be a bit late but it's never too late for God. He loves us and waits for us to say we are sorry and then He can put us back on the right road again."

Dippy was thinking of his Mum back home and all the times that she had told him to do things but he didn't do them when she asked. Jonah had taught him a lesson that day, to always do what is right and good even if it isn't what you feel like doing.

"Look," said Dippy "There's the ship we were on, they must have come back, because of the storm."

So Jonah and Dippy walked across to the ship and to their surprise there wasn't any one there.

"They must have gone into town to get some food," said Jonah.

Jonah and Dippy were no longer afraid of the men.

So Dippy Dan took Jonah's hand and led him onto the ship to where his time machine had landed and began searching for his BGTM remote, crawling around on his hands and knees in the storeroom, looking everywhere for more than an hour.

Jonah just stood and watched. Dippy might just as well have been looking for a small needle in a haystack because there was nothing to be found and then he shouted,

"Yes! Here it is!" it was on the floor under an old sack and so Dippy showed Noah, who didn't seem impressed.

Dippy climbed up onto the boxes and sat down.

"See, I told you that I have a time machine."

"Sure Dippy, don't worry lad," he said shaking his head in disbelief and smiling.

Dippy smiled at his friend Jonah from up above.

"Ok, watch this then Mr. Clever Noah, replied Dippy. "You'll see and then maybe you'll believe me!"

And after resetting his BGTM remote, there right in front of them both appeared his time machine, to Jonah's amazement and shock.

"Forgive me for not believing you Dippy, I can see now that you were telling me the truth," said Noah.

"Don't worry Noah; it was never going to be easy to believe that I have a time machine... now you know!"

The two friends hugged and Dippy went inside his BGTM promising he would come back to see Jonah one day, while Jonah stood back and waved him goodbye. Then …whoosh he was gone.

Seconds later Dippy Dan arrived back home in his Dippy cave and because he was away from home for many days, he needed to set his time machine to get back home seconds after he left just in case anyone noticed he had gone so that he would still get some sleep and be in time for breakfast in the morning!

"Clever ol time machine eh?" Mumbled Dippy under his breath then climbed back into his tent and went off to sleep as though he'd never left his Dippy cave at all. Wouldn't you like to have a BGTM?

Guess what Dippy was dreaming about? Yep you got it, his next adventure but he knew that he would miss his friend Jonah who had taught him so much.

When the morning came Dippy yawned and stretched his arms, opened his big double doors and walked into the house whistling.

"Hi Mum," he said and sat down for his breakfast.

"Did you sleep well Dippy?" his Mum asked,

"I slept like a Time Traveller Mum," Dippy said, smiling to himself and only we know why!

After breakfast Dippy's Mum asked him,

"What are you doing today?" Dippy replied,

"Oh nothing much Mum, maybe I will go back to the Stone Age and show them an easier way to carry water." Dippy's Mummy looked confused but smiled and said,

"Get on with you Dippy, just keep out of trouble and don't forget to use the sun cream because it's going to be hot today," "No worries Mum," he said.

Dippy can hardly contain his excitement, as he plans to change the past by taking something from the future to a very special family and guess who else is excited?

Chapter Nine

Dippy ran off out into the garden and even though his Mummy didn't believe he was going to go back to the Stone Age, he knew that was exactly where he was going and be back in time for his lunch!

"Now where did I see that big water barrel that Dad uses when we go on holiday in the caravan, it will be perfect for Oggia's Mummy to get the water from the river," mumbled Dippy and as he opened the doors of his Dippy cave, there it was standing against the wall.

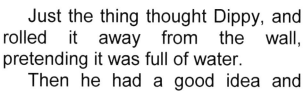 Just the thing thought Dippy, and rolled it away from the wall, pretending it was full of water.

Then he had a good idea and quickly ran back indoors and emptied his colouring box onto the floor, collected up all his crayons and found a big colouring book.

"Oggia will love this," he said out loud and ran down to the kitchen to get some sandwiches and biscuits to take with him on his journey back to the Stone Age.

Suddenly Dippy's brother Dylan appeared at the doors of his Dippy cave and said,

"Can you come and play football with me Dippy?" But Dippy was too busy to go and play football, besides he was worried that Dylan would want to go for a ride in his BGTM there and then and said,

"Ok but only for a while," so Dippy went out into the yard to play football with his brother Dylan and they both kicked the ball about for a while but then Dippy saw his chance to escape and kicked the ball over the next-door neighbour's garden,

"Oh blow it," said Dippy, "That sorts that out, now we haven't got a ball." Dylan began crying and shouted, "Muuum, Dippy has kicked my football over the fence," but his Mummy couldn't hear him and then Dippy saw his chance to get away from his little brother.

"Hey Dylan," he said, "Would you like to play on my new roller skates?" "Cool," said Dylan and ran off into the house to get them.

"Phew that was close," muttered Dippy,

"Now to get back to my BGTM and prepare to go back to see Oggia and her Mummy."

When Dippy got back to his Dippy cave, he rolled the Caravan water barrel over to his time machine and stood it in front of the controls, suddenly a voice called out,

"Dippy where are you?" Dippy had to think quickly, closed the door of his BGTM and ran outside to meet his Dad.

His Dad had come to ask if Dippy wanted to go fishing with him.

"Ah, hi Dad," said Dippy, "Look Dad I'm a bit busy at the moment sorting out my Dippy cave but I will go fishing with you tomorrow if you want?"

Dippy tried not to sound too suspicious and then his Dad answered,

"So what are you so busy doing?" Dippy Dan knew that if he told his Daddy a fib he wouldn't believe him so he said,

"Erm, well I am going back to the Stone Age to help my friend Oggia and her Mummy find a better way of getting water from the river." Dippy's Dad laughed and said,

"Sure Dippy, don't worry have a lovely afternoon." And walked off laughing and muttering loudly,

"Stone Age? that's so funny Dippy, you are so funny son."

When the coast was clear, Dippy pulled the big brown double doors of his Dippy cave shut hoping that no one else would disturb him.

As Dippy got back inside his time machine he sat for a moment thinking of Oggia and Oggia's Mummy and all the lovely people he could meet and also all the exciting places he could go to. What an amazing time machine I have, he thought.

If only his Mummy knew her son was a Time Traveller with his very own BGTM!

"Time to go," muttered Dippy and off he went back to see his little friend Oggia, thousands and thousands of years back in time to the Stone Age.

Moments later Dippy's BFTM had landed back inside Oggia's cave but this time things were different and Dippy was in for a big surprise!

Oggia's Mummy was getting their dinner ready while little Oggia stood in the cave entrance and shouted, "Ippy Yan! Ippy Yan!" in happiness to see her new friend Dippy again but suddenly out from the corner of the cave came a wild red headed cave woman screaming, with a sharp pointed spear in her hand but to Dippy's relief, Oggia's Mummy was able to tell her in Cave language that all was well and that Dippy is Oggia's friend.

Dippy could see that it was Oggia's Auntie and soon they were all smiling at him and offered him some of their food which made Dippy laugh because it was a massive Mammoth leg or something but he ate some of it just to be polite.

"Maybe I should ask Mummy if I can have a Mammoth joint when I get back home," Dippy giggled to himself.

Dippy rolled the water barrel over to Oggia's Mummy and wondered how he was going to explain to her and Oggia how to use it but then he thought of a good idea, as Dippy often does!

He thought that if he could take the water barrel down to the river then he could show Oggia's Mummy how to fill it up and she could roll it back up to their cave. So, Dippy took Oggia by the hand and pointed to the river while leading her and her Mummy and Auntie down to the river side.

Dippy was so excited that he was doing something for these lovely people by making their lives so much easier.

"Come on," he said, "follow me and I will show you what to do." The river was just in front of them and thankfully there wasn't anyone else there.

Dippy grabbed the big plastic screw at the top of the water barrel and began to turn it round and round until it fell off in his hand.

Oggia's Mummy came to look inside it and Dippy couldn't help laughing at this lovely cave woman who had no idea what he was about to do.

Dippy Dan's trip back in time to the Stone Age makes him very happy, especially when he gets down to the river with Oggia. Perhaps Dippy is in love!

Chapter Ten

So Dippy Dan showed Oggia's Mummy how to fill the water barrel up and also how to pull it along, she was so happy that now she didn't have to drag that big heavy animal skin full of water up from the river and back to her cave.

Dippy and Oggia stood there smiling at one another and it didn't matter that they couldn't really understand each other because the smiles said it all.

Oggia's Auntie rested on a large rock and smiled.

So Dippy, Oggia, her Mummy and Oggia's Auntie went back up to their cave, with Oggia's Mummy happily driving the big water barrel to her home.

Sadly, it was then time for Dippy to go his home and Oggia stood next to Dippy in his big green time machine while Oggia's Mummy zoomed around the cave with her new water barrel laughing and singing.

Dippy wished that he could take them back home with him but it would be so hard for them to live in a world with televisions, airplanes, houses and even McDonalds!

Dippy could see that Oggia and her mummy both wanted him to stay with them but Dippy knew that wouldn't be possible and hoped that somehow he would see these lovely simple cave people again one day soon. Then Dippy remembered the sandwiches and biscuits he had brought with him and the little camera from inside his BGTM door pouch and off he went to get them.

Oggia, her Mummy and her Auntie were wondering what he was going to do and then out came Dippy Dan again to take a photo of them all.

He wanted to have their photo so that he could remember them when he got back home and to put their photo next to his bed so that he could see their happy smiling faces.

But Oggia's Auntie refused to have her photo taken so Oggia and her Mummy stood together smiling while Dippy took their picture.

Dippy smiled at himself when he brought out his colouring books and crayons, it made Dippy so happy to know that these lovely people would enjoy them wondering what these three lovely cave people will think of these unusual toys. I can't imagine what they would think if they saw my XBox or my mobile Smart phone, thought Dippy.

Dippy gave them the colouring books and after just a few times showing Oggia how to colour in the pictures, she was away copying Dippy, using the crayons and colouring inside the lines around the pictures. Even Oggia's Mummy and Auntie had a go and they laughed and giggled at each other.

Dippy opened his little blue lunchbox and shared his sandwiches and biscuits with them. It was such a special moment which Dippy didn't ever want to end.

But it was time to go home so, after lots of hugs, Dippy waved goodbye to Oggia, her Auntie and her Mummy and zoomed off through time, thousands of years into the future back to his home in Carltonville.

When Dippy arrived inside his Dippy cave again he quickly covered over his time machine with the big brown tarpaulin and scampered into the house to have his dinner and waiting there by the door was his Mummy, who said jokingly,

"Well Dippy, you managed to get back home in time for dinner for a change, have you had a nice day, darling?" His Daddy stood there too.

Dippy wanted to tell her but Dippy was sure that even if he told them the truth his Mummy and Daddy wouldn't believe him and answered,

"Yep, I have had a lovely time with Oggia and her family, they are from the Stone Age, then said,

"I went there last week and mended Oggia's stone dog but then I went back today to show Oggia's Mummy a better way of getting water up from the river."

Dippy Dan's Mum and Dad smiled at each other and his Mummy said,

"Did you show them how to make a round wheel too, Dippy?" and they all began laughing and Dippy laughed with them because he knew they didn't believe a word he said but he wasn't worried, it was such fun seeing them laugh.

That night Dippy lay in bed with his eyes almost closing, day-dreaming of the amazing adventures he had been on in his BGTM. The morning would bring new adventures but with Dippy so very tired he was just glad to be in his own bed and not inside the belly of a smelly Whale! He closed his eyes, fell asleep and slept like a log!

And there on his bedside cabinet was the photo he had taken of Oggia and her Mummy, to remind him of the wonderful time he had with them.

Would he go back and visit his lovely little friend?

THE END

Shhh, it's not really the end because there's another adventure coming soon and I hope you join me then? Bye for now and I will hopefully see you again. Dippy Dan.

Just remember not to do anything I wouldn't do!

We hope you enjoyed this Dippy Dan adventure.

For further information or to place an order,
please contact our Office Administrator below.

Email: info@dippydanbooks.com
Website: www.dippydanbooks.com

Facebook: @DippyDanBooks
Twitter: @DippyDanBooks

Other adventures in this series:

Dippy in the Ark

Dippy and Goliath

Dippy and the Whale

Dippy in the Lion's den

Dippy on the Gospel road

Dippy in the Garden of Eden

Many more Adventures in the Dippy Pipeline

20722210R00035

Printed in Great Britain
by Amazon